SID
THE SO SAD
Skeleton

Written by Kelly Jeppesen and Illustrated by Ryan Jeppesen

About the Author

Kelly and his wife Andrea enjoy teaching and reading children's books to their five young kids. Sometimes Kelly tells stories about monsters, and occasionally a story gets elaborate enough that he has to ask his brother Ryan to illustrate it for him. He is very grateful for Ryan's help and Andrea's support.

When he's not at home helping Andrea with the kids, Kelly goes to work as a small town doctor. Like the doctor in *Sid the So-Sad Skeleton*, Kelly sees plenty of people whose conditions can't be fixed with medicines. Unlike Sid's doctor though, Kelly has never had the privilege of treating the undead in his practice.

About the Illustrator

Ryan and his wife Brooke have their hands full raising four not-so-little-anymore monsters. Between working full-time, coaching football, painting, wood carving, sculpting, playing board games, and bread baking, Ryan sometimes finds time to illustrate children's books.

While it is true that his brother Kelly got the brains in the family, Kelly's stick figure drawings were atrocious. But he's a doctor, so in the end he wins. So, Ryan was very happy to help his little brother on this fun project. For his next project, Ryan plans on building a life-size gargoyle to guard the entrance to his home.

Text © 2016 Kelly Jeppesen
Illustrations © 2016 Ryan Jeppesen

ISBN 978-1533074485

Sid the Skeleton was so, so sad. He did not have any friends.

"I know!" said Sid. "I will be a friend with Wanda the Witch!"

"You can be my friend," said Wanda, "if you give me some hair for my potion."

Wanda looked
all around Sid.

NOPE.
NO HAIR.

Sid went to the doctor.
"I am so, so sad," said Sid.
"I need a cream
so I can grow hair."

He got the cream,
but it did not work.

Sid was still
so sad.

"I know!" said Sid. "I will be a friend with Vinny the Vampire instead!"

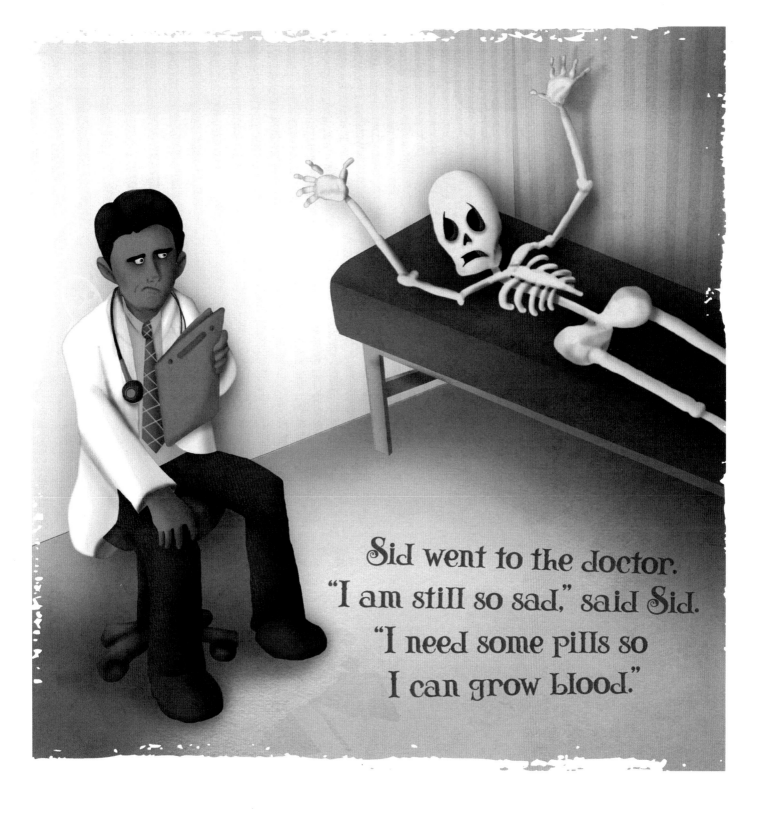

Sid went to the doctor.
"I am still so sad," said Sid.
"I need some pills so
I can grow blood."

He got the pills,
but they did
not work.

Sid was
still
so,
so
sad.

"I know!" said Sid. "I will be a a friend with Zeb and Zac, the zombies!"

"You can be our friend,"
said Zeb, "if you give us some brains."
Zac just said "BrAiNs!" really loud.

Zeb and Zac looked all around Sid.

NOPE.
NO BRAINS.

"I have tried!" said Sid. "But I do not have what the other monsters want from their friends."

Sid went to the pet store.

The fish were scared of him.

The cats were scared of him.

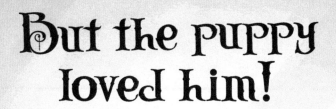

But the PUPPY loved him!

He went to pay for the PUPPY.

Puppy for sale!

The clerk was
also scared
of him.

Sid loved his new puppy.

And the puppy loved Sid just the way he was.

Sid the Skeleton
was so, so happy.

And the other monsters were so, so jealous.

Made in the USA
Las Vegas, NV
21 October 2020